MIRACLES FROM HEAVEN

A MINI MEMOIR

By Rev. Dr. Florence Fraser

Miracles from Heaven—A Mini Memoir

Trilogy Christian Publishers A Wholly Owned Subsidiary of Trinity Broadcasting Network

2442 Michelle Drive Tustin, CA 92780

Trilogy Christian Publishing/TBN and colophon are trademarks of Trinity Broadcasting Network.

Cover design by: Malcolm C. Fraser, Sr.

For information about special discounts for bulk purchases, please contact Trilogy Christian Publishing.

Trilogy Disclaimer: The views and content expressed in this book are those of the author and may not necessarily reflect the views and doctrine of Trilogy Christian Publishing or the Trinity Broadcasting Network.

Manufactured in the United States of America

10 9 8 7 6 5 4 3 2 1

Library of Congress Cataloging-in-Publication Data is available.

ISBN: 978-1-68556-787-3

E-ISBN: 978-1-68556-788-0

ACKNOWLEDGMENTS

I give all honor and glory to God, who encouraged me every step of the way as I wrote this book!

Thanks to Philippians 4:13 (NKJV) that taught me, "I can do all things through Christ who strengthens me," and all those who kept inspiring me to "write a book."

Much appreciation to my nieces—Dr. Terri Belgrave and aspiring Dr. Tawi Castello— for not giving up on me but waiting patiently for me to get this book out. Also, to all my other nieces and nephews for inspiring me to "put it in a book!"

I will always be indebted to all those who mentored, coached, and counseled me along this journey. These include siblings Malcolm Fraser, Merlene Castello, Sis. Pat Clarke, Elizabeth Fraser, and Joy Blanchard. For honorable mention, I must include the late Dr. S. Ovid Isaacs, Bro. Burnell Fields and their spouses, as well as my late parents Malcolm C and Albertha V. Fraser.

Thanks to all of you for inspiring me!

TABLE OF CONTENTS

THE MID-TIMES

CAMPS AND SHENANIGANS

INTRODUCTION

Not many people believe in miracles. They feel these were experiences in Bible days that are left in the past. On the contrary, I am here to propose to you that miracles still happen in our day. As seen in the incidents related in this book, you will see that I have experienced multiple miracles, and I pray that you will allow yourself the faith and grace to experience some also.

I began this book with the intention of sharing some of my exciting life experiences with my nieces and nephews but foresee that it would be a good read and a form of encouragement and blessing to many others.

Go ahead and dive in to see for yourself and use your own faith, even as small as a grain of mustard seed, to realize your own miracles and grow your faith!

Matthew 17:20 (KJV) says, "Jesus said unto them...if ye have faith as a grain of mustard seed, ye shall say unto this mountain, remove hence to yonder place; and it shall remove; and nothing shall be impossible unto you."

Are you dealing with some seemingly impossible situations?

I pray that by the time you're through reading this small volume, your faith will be increased to move those mountains just like I've seen done on my journey since my teenage years.

Enjoy!

Chapter 1

Guyana Conditional Scholarship

"Good news!" Here was a clear opportunity to pursue your life goals. I just got wind that the government was making scholarships available for individuals to merge their goals with that of the authorities, resulting in benefits to both! Little did I know this was not going to be a straightforward, cut-and-dry process...

On inquiry, I learned of the requirements for obtaining the scholarship and was excited to find that I met the stipulations based on the knowledge of my qualifications and my goals and desires for "giving back." Basically, applicants needed to have obtained a specific number of G.C.E., *O Level* subjects, have a desire, and/or agree to serve their country for five years after completing studies in a needed field. For this, you would have to sign a contract.

From an early age, I have had a strong interest in helping people as a psychologist, and this was a very scarce field in the country. I had no knowledge of any professional psychologists. On doing some research, I found that the scarcity was very real. So I decided this was my sure opportunity to make a major difference. It warmed my heart to submit my application with necessary supporting documents and felt good thinking, *For sure, I have this in the bag!* But lo and behold, I received a response from the scholarship committee stating that my application was denied. This answer certainly was not the response I expected, and I was very discouraged...to the extent that, despite my quiet nature and demeanor, I decided to discuss this latest development with my youth leader.

My youth leader was a gentleman of strong faith who believed in miracles, standing tall for what you believed and pursuing your dreams and goals with determination as you prayed fervently about the matter. So this is exactly what we did. Further, this man of God encouraged me to take necessary action to determine a different, more positive response from the scholarship committee. Now, we were very aware that other individuals with similar qualifications had successfully obtained scholarships in their fields of choice resulting in this matter now having an appearance of some discrimination, which would rob the country of the benefits in my field of choice.

We decided to write a letter to the scholarship committee with a carbon copy to the president of the country since he himself was the Chief Officer in the Ministry responsible for government scholarships. In a short time, I received a response from the President's Office, inviting me to an interview with the President himself. Coached by that strong, sincere man of God, with much prayer and fasting, I prepared for that notorious meeting with the President. At this time, I definitely felt like a *Daniel in the lion's den* since neither myself nor my family had any special political ties. But on approaching the gate to the President's Office, my dad stopped the car to announce our appointment to a response of great respect as the gates were immediately swung open to let us in. That felt like the first rung of victory. After some other preliminaries of a security nature, we were sitting face to face with the late, great President Lyndon Forbes Sampson Burnham. Surprisingly, the President was very cordial, respectful, and humane in his approach. He asked legitimate questions in engaging my parent and me about my school career, accomplishments, and then the current goal with regard to the Government Conditional Scholarship in question. In some ways, the President seemed apologetic that the matter of my gaining one of the coveted scholarships had to come before him. But by the end of our meeting, he noted I would be hearing from his office and scholarship committee. He presented himself as a fair and just human being.

In a short time thereafter, I received final approval for a Guyana Conditional Scholarship to study Psychology. I knew for sure that God still works miracles and that this was one. It was a true miracle from heaven and one of many to come. I bowed my head and thanked God. I thanked my youth leader—a stalwart of a believer who was instrumental in my pursuing my goals and letting God Himself take the leadership role! He fights our battles, and He is faithful. This was a sure victory over the wiles of the enemy. Due to this development, many have benefited from my counseling skills and experience as a psychologist. Faithful to my contract, I gave back multiple years in excess of the five years contracted to my country before leaving for the mission field and pursuing further studies in my chosen field.

Chapter 2

COLLEGE ACCEPTANCE

Time to select an institution of higher learning. *Where would I receive a quality education in my program?* I thought. I went to our home library, where Dad had a collection of Webster's Encyclopedias, and set about searching for colleges and universities. Wow...there were Christian colleges too! I looked these over back and forth, closed my eyes, said a prayer, and picked one. It was Bridgewater College—the very first private, co-educational four-year college in the Commonwealth of Virginia. On closer examination, I learned that this was a small college under the oversight of the Brethren Church. Now, this last bit of information caught my attention because the church I attended was of the Brethren denomination. This was now adding to the excitement of my school search project. I earnestly delved more into the history of this school and its requirements. Before long, I was in touch with the school enquiring about admission and submitted my application as a foreign student. Much of my communication was through the United States Consulate in Georgetown, Guyana.

The officials in both institutions were very cordial and professional. I was happy to see that when I negotiated a waiver of the TOEFL exam, the administrators were readily accepting. This was an examination to verify the student could communicate fluently in English. Since Guyana was a former British Colony and the only English-speaking country on the mainland in South America, it was not difficult to convince school personnel that communication and learning would not be hindered by immediate understanding. The necessary documentation was completed, and this hurdle was soon behind us.

Now I was scanning the mail daily for responses from Bridgewater College. I continually rehearsed that I had completed all documents, including my essay, and submitted the same. Why did it now seem to be taking forever for a final response? And then it came! It was on a wet, dreary day, so the appearance and welcoming content of that mail immediately brightened everything that memorable day. Simply put, the college mail stated Bridgewater College was happy to assure me an open place on their Foreign Student roster. This was one of the best days of my life. Another miracle had taken place for which I've been extremely grateful, resulting in a permanent smile at every remembrance!

Chapter 3

FAMILY AWAY FROM HOME

"Oh, Florence, you speak such good British English!" was my frequent greeting from friends and now family while I was thousands of miles away from home. It was mid-November. I had slept in my cousin's oversized coat and blankets and comforters from Rowena, Rhonda, and their friends down the hall. These young women had opened their hearts to a newcomer in the midst of the cold fall weather and a broken boiler on campus. That was my first night at Bridgewater College!

Delise was walking me around campus now and, of course, voiced her surprise that I did not speak Spanish. She had dreaded what our interaction would be like before realizing I spoke fluent "British English!" Now we were back in the dorms, and the welcome was overwhelming. Everyone wanted to talk with me. Row and Rhonda wanted me to come home with them in ten days. What was I doing for Thanksgiving? Interestingly, they found I was a more quiet, reticent individual, the *new kid on the block*, yet they were treating me like family... This was definitely a Christian college, and so it remained!

Situation after situation proved I now had a much more extended family at the small Baptist church I now attended and that with folk on campus. Naomi and George Flory took me under their wings and served as substitute parents with me so many thousands of miles away from home. They would continue doing the same when I returned to the area twenty years later as a college professor at a nearby community college. Naomi drove me around for hours car hunting, and Mr. Flory taught me everything I needed to know about my auto maintenance, including timely decals from DMV. He even showed me how to test and change my oil. As time went on, the couple shared with me from their kitchen garden. It was always a welcome sight to often be greeted by plump red tomatoes with a note left outside my door along with a copy of the daily newspaper. You immediately knew either one was there while you were out. They were such a total blessing!

On the occasion of the Florys' 50th wedding anniversary, another guest asked me, "Are you kin?" I was quite tickled, and Naomi and I shared the funny joke for a long time after I told her I must be their "long lost cousin, who spent so much time in Florida, I got a good tan!"

Another pair of godsends were Earl and Debbie Smith, who attended our church but who became much better known to me as my landlord and lady. When I went to rent their two-bedroom apartment, Earl recognized me as a choir member. I felt that was easy for him since I was the sole Black member of the church. When I sought permission to share space with someone to help maintain rent payments, Earl said, "Florence, I'd rather you didn't do that...if you run into problems, I'd work with you." And that he did. In 1992, the college began downsizing and cut back my hours hence affecting my ability to meet rent payments. On sharing this predicament with Earl, he answered, "Florence, tell me your plan, and I'll cooperate with you." He was just so encouraging and compassionate. Both Earl and Debbie were extremely neighborly when eight members of my family visited from New York City, and nine of us filled up a pew at church. Naomi and I laughed to note they had never seen that many Black people in all their lives. The Smiths came to meet and greet my family bearing a sumptuous loaf of zucchini bread and were happy to grant the young kids tractor and horse rides around their expansive farmyard!

These kind deeds were topped when I, myself, had to return to NYC owing rent, and Earl let me make regular payments until I was completely paid up. Earl was so happy to celebrate this with others because he felt I was true to my commitment, and he wanted to celebrate the integrity of a young Black person as he had *never seen before*!

Yet other remarkable families included the Puffenbargers, who gathered furniture for me as I needed to move from a furnished to an unfurnished rental apartment. Paul exclaimed, "Florence, everything came together like it was supposed to be!" He went on to explain that visitors, seeing the collected household items at their home, would enquire about them and when told they were for me, they were stimulated to add to the collection. Pastor Kelly Lane and the Bridgewater Baptist Church Family Group, who collaborated in moving and setting these furnishings up in my new place, seemed tireless in doing their great good. The home that greeted me when they brought me there would appear to any onlooker that I had gone out and made all these purchases myself. The way the home was so well coordinated and matching...All this was evidence to Paul that I was sent... I did not just come. Little did he know that I had been called directly by God and assigned missionary to New York and the uttermost parts of the world, including the United States. Further, on arriving at a local church to do a film presentation for Underground Evangelism, I was greeted by the question: "Are you the missionary?"

Multiple other families took care of me as their own while I was away from home. These included the Browns, the Scales, the Connors, the Dells, the Ulrichs, the Laymans, and the McCarthy families. While Helen and I would spend special moments sharing about things of God, and she fed me her best Southern home-cooked meals, now Evangelist Freda spent long hours ensuring my hair was well done and I was appropriately groomed. These were my best friends and newly found family. Only, I pray they know how much I appreciated them and all they did because back then, I was too quiet in my demeanor.

Chapter 4

MEMBERSHIPS

Despite my quiet nature, I participated in multiple organizations. These, too, provided family support for me. They included the Student Committee on Religious Activities (SCRA), in which I served as Chair of the Crisis Committee, Students Interested in Relating to the Church (SIRCH), the Brethren Church group, the French Club, the concert choir, and the oratorio. We met on a weekly basis in these groups and often went on camping trip meetings. In the spring semester, the concert choir toured Virginia and neighboring states, and the oratorio sang Handel's Messiah at Christmas. These interactions generated numerous pleasant memories.

On one concert choir trip, I sat next to Prof. Trout, our music director. In the ensuing conversation, Prof. Trout stated, "Florence, you are one of the older students, aren't you?!" He went on to explain, "You look young like the rest of them, but when I talk with you, I can tell you're older. Your maturity rings through... " Well, that made my day for a long time, although I already knew that I looked younger than I was. Should we make trips today, I would sit with Prof. Trout again and again!

These trips on tour revealed a lot to me. I had never realized you could gain weight in just one weekend. The sumptuous spread with Sloppy Joes, potato salad, various pies, and multiple other tasty dishes at our different tour stops caused me to gain as much as five pounds in one weekend! This realization quickly taught me how to get a little of everything without overcrowding my plate and being ever so mindful of the types of food I consumed on concert choir trips.

The hosts all wanted to provide their best spread for us guests. These tours also taught me strength, dignity, and perseverance in the face of challenges. In the midst of one concert presentation, inclement weather developed, resulting in a power outage; but without much ado, the host quickly provided a massive amount of candles, and we finished the concert by beautiful, romantic candlelight and *a cappella* tones—a remarkable impromptu presentation!

Other unforgettable experiences include Easter sunrise services at Dr. David Metzler's homestead with the SIRCH group. It was awesome to witness the gorgeous sunrise as we lustily sang, "He arose the victor from the dark domain, and He lives forever with His saints to reign. He arose. He arose. Hallelujah, Christ arose... " Competing with these activities were our foreign students' gatherings at Dr. and Mrs. Ellsworth Kyger's home. They seemed to go all out to make us feel comfortable and well supported while attending school so many thousands of miles away from home. Thanks for all you did for us. We shall forever be indebted to you and graciously thank you! Let me say thanks also to you, SIRCH and SCRA campers, who let me lay on the sofa with my comforter while you stretched out in sleeping bags on the floor at the Reich Cabin. In addition, thanks to the leadership and members of the Black Students Society for all you did to include and make me feel a part of your group, although I did not say much nor know how to dance. To my little sister, Reat, I missed you when you left and will always feel that bond with you. Thank you for being family.

Chapter 5

Bird International Pick Up

On one occasion, I had flown to Guyana on vacation and had an arrangement to fly back to campus. In the midst of all this, there was some last-minute change of schedule with the airline whereby I could no longer get a connecting flight to Virginia. I made multiple calls to Student Services Department on campus, explained my situation, and requested pick-up in Washington, D.C. The counselor promised to check into this, and I promised to call back for a response.

As the time drew closer to my return trip, I made several calls to campus in an effort to follow up but could never get an answer on the phone. So the day for me to travel came, and I had no idea whether or not someone would pick me up at Bird International Airport in Washington, D.C., where the new travel arrangement was taking me. All this while, I offered up several prayers for God to help me with this dilemma. Without this help, I was perplexed concerning how I would get from Washington to Virginia. I decided I'll have to "walk by faith and not by sight" (2 Corinthians 5:7).

The date for travel arrived with still no feedback from campus; everyone was now on vacation. It was one of the break periods. I had my suitcase packed and boarded the plane in Guyana, made a brief stop in the Caribbean, and by sundown, we were at Bird International. It was time to think of continuing to travel again, and I said a prayer. I recall being pretty calm and seemed to hear a voice say, "Help is on the way..." I did not see anyone, nor could I fathom how this would develop. Nevertheless, I put my small suitcase to the side and walked back to lug the larger one over and managed to pull that also over into the corner. Then I breathed a word of thanks and waited.

I remember being pretty calm during this strange phenomenon despite not knowing what would happen and what I would do should no one come when I saw a familiar figure approaching me. It was my very good friend, Mike Scales, a student counselor from campus. Boy, was I glad to see him; but it was when he told the story of how he came to be there that I realized that this was a true miracle. Reportedly, he had overheard the telephone conversation about me needing help and did not know if someone would get me. So since he was on assignment in the area that weekend, he decided to take the responsibility to check on me himself in case no one else came. And there I was, waiting!

By Mike's own report, he felt very privileged and blessed to be "the chosen one." And on my own account, I was so grateful and thanked God for hearing and answering my prayers in such a miraculous way. I thought, *Miracles from heaven!*

Chapter 6

ONE WEEK—THAT'S ALL

Thirteen years after graduating from Bridgewater College, I decided to return to the area for a visit. I had recently completed my master's degree in Psychology and thought, *Why not pay a visit, reunite with friends, and scout the job market to see what prospects I might find?* I had had an excellent four-year experience there in my college days and thought this might be a worthwhile exploration.

I got on the phone with a couple of friends. Anita, my old roommate, was scheduled to pick me up at the Amtrak Station in Arlington, Virginia. Then I'll connect with Naomi, who arranged for me to stay in the dorms on campus since it was the summer break, and most of the students were gone. That seemed like a good base and workstation.

On the day of travel, I joined the Amtrak at Penn Station in New York City and made the uneventful eight-hour trip to Arlington, Virginia. This trip was different for me because back in the day, I traveled on the Greyhound. But the train ride was peaceful and enjoyable. Anita and her husband, Gilmer, along with their four-year-old Christopher and months old Aaron, met me at the train. It was a meeting and a greeting after all these years, but we soon got to their home, ate dinner, visited a while, and prepared to settle down for the night. Then a very remarkable, memorable thing happened. Anita asked young Christopher who he would like to tuck him in that night: her or "Aunt Flo?" And without hesitation, he said, "Aunt Flo." Well, that certainly made my day, and thereafter, Christopher became my very special nephew! The next day, they put me on the

Greyhound to Naomi in Bridgewater. It was such a good feeling being back in the country after all these years... felt like old times!

Naomi picked me up in Harrisonburg, Virginia, took me to eat, and that was the start of a very enjoyable full week. I visited with old friends, including professors on campus, and rekindled old bonds. Prof. Kent (Psychology Department Chair) and Dr. Don Witters (my old Psychology Major Advisor) were so elated to see me, and I had to fill each in on all I had been doing in the in-between years. No sooner had I let Prof. Kent know I was looking at the job market than he posted me over to the Psychology Department Chair at James Madison University in Harrisonburg to see if they had openings. Since they had already filled their positions, the Chair, in turn, referred me with high recommendations to Blue Ridge Community College, where they needed an adjunct professor in Psychology, as well as a Black student mentor and advisor. Without much ado, I interviewed for these two positions and received positive feedback concerning the prospects.

All the while, Naomi Flory let me use her home as the office base from where I made phone calls, and she took me to every appointment. She also presented me with the newspapers every day, so I could keep abreast of the news and look up other possible job openings. Just like back in my college days, Naomi and her husband, George, took me under their wings and provided the substitute parenting that any adult child would appreciate. In addition, we often laughed at Naomi's efforts to find me a husband when Mr. Flory would have to tell her, "Naomi, maybe Florence is okay the way she is."

Before we knew it, the week was over, and I was heading back to New York, having accomplished my goals of visiting and reuniting with friends, as well as obtaining at least one and possibly two jobs that could work alongside each other. I later returned to assume the adjunct professor position since they hired a Black minister of the Gospel for mentoring and advising their Black student body. That was okay with me. All it took was one week—that's all!

Chapter 7

THE HOME RENTAL

I had rented a furnished apartment for approximately a year when I felt the need to get a new regular apartment. Friends and I did the usual networking. We scoured the newspapers. Each time, we came up empty. Then one day, I saw an entry that seemed promising. On that same day, I consulted with Joyce, the secretary at the college, and she pointed out the same entry I had seen. So we decided to call the telephone number listed to make an appointment to view the apartment. It was a new two-bedroom facility on Penny Layne in close proximity to Bridgewater, being rented by Earl Smith.

On the day of the appointment, I arrived very timely and met with Mr. Smith. He was very cordial, polite, and happy to show me his place in one of his two new buildings. This was his last unit to be rented. In the midst of the tour, Mr. Smith surprised me. "Do you sing in the choir down at the Baptist Church, Florence?" he asked. When I answered in the affirmative, he smiled and continued, "I thought I had seen you somewhere before." Thus, in the conversation that now ensued, I learned that he and his wife Debbie were new members of the church I attended. We both expressed our surprise by simultaneously exclaiming, "What a small world!"

It was a beautiful apartment with an attractive living room and spacious bedrooms. The open design parquet floor plan against the white kitchen tiles and panels made it feel larger and airier. Now we had seen the place and discussed the cost, which was relatively reasonable, but just to be sure of maintaining, I asked would he mind if I shared the apartment with someone else. He declined but added,

29

"Florence, if you come up against any problems, please tell me, and I'll cooperate with you." Happy to say, this was the beginning of a dear and viable relationship between my family and me and the Smiths.

The three years spent in this home were no less than *wonderful*! The Smiths treated me like family. When my folks visited from New York, Debbie brought over some delicious zucchini bread—a very heartwarming gesture. Mr. Smith showed my brother his horses and gave the children rides on the horses and the tractor, as well as let them look at his cows up close. My brother found his visit quite delightful because he was a horse lover and retired mounted police back in my homeland. When rental payment challenges arose due to the downsizing of my hours at the college, true to his word, Mr. Smith worked it out with me.

Notably, I relocated back to New York because I could not find suitable work to supplement my income. Mr. Smith allowed me to pay him as I was able until my bill was completely paid. We have kept in touch to date and are always happy to reunite by phone and/or in person. I count this experience a true blessing along life's journey and a miracle from God!

A Preamble

Chapter 8

A QUIET SHY "LAST ROW"

"Has anyone seen Rita?" They called me Rita to honor my aunt. I was right there but so quiet and shy as a kitten. My mom recalled I had that disposition, practically, as it were from birth. As a young child in arms, I avoided people's kisses, and as an older child, I would wipe the kisses away. For this reason, an uncle nicknamed me "Keesh" after a character of the same mannerisms in a calypso of the day.

For a very long time (nine years), I was the last of five children born to my parents. When people did not expect to have more children, they referred fondly to the last one as their "last row." I carried that title until we got my baby sister, Joy, but the effects of this position stayed with me for years to come. In addition, my quiet, shy behavior also remained late into my life. Some relatives and friends did not know me as well as they knew my siblings because when visitors arrived, I retreated to my bedroom with a book. This probably contributed to more shyness because when I spoke, I sounded like a book which in turn caused me to remain quiet so as not to sound so different to peers.

This quiet, shy behavior no doubt worked for and against me. On the one hand, I was considered a coveted well-behaved child that was any parent's dream. Even in my childhood days, parents saw the blessing of having a child that does not have a behavior problem. On the other hand, this behavior prevented me from participating even when I dearly wanted to do so, for example, in class and at camp activities. It was almost crippling and caused me many disappointments.

Later in life, no one knew what angst it cost me to stand before a university class of fifty to teach. But look at me now, even daring to write about it... Well, glory to God! I must say, I learned a lot about myself while teaching those classes. At camp, in my teenage years, I would have something I wanted to share during the "quiet time" session, but due to shyness, I could not do so. Then someone else would share the same idea, and having missed my chance, I would have to think of something else to share, and often, it was too late. Imagine what a vicious cycle this became in multiple places needing public expression.

Well, I can still be quiet, but I'm so over the shyness now that I think sometimes people would rather I sat out and did not share a thing. As for me, *they don't know where the Lord has brought me from and that in itself is a miracle!*

Chapter 9

TEACHER'S PET

Being the quiet, well-behaved child I was, it is no wonder that I was often considered the *teacher's pet*. I would sit right up in the front row of seats in class. I did not volunteer much, but I paid strict attention and answered if called. I got good grades with full scores in my classes and topped the class consecutively. For this, I won the respect of my fellow classmates, and some would refer to me for help with homework questions. As for teachers, their pet phrase on my report cards was "a pleasure to teach." And if my score was ninety-nine percent out of one hundred, they had to account for the missing one percent because I worked hard for every single percent of my grade. On one occasion, my teacher's explanation for one missing point was that he had to search for some reason to not give me that point, so I did not think that I'd arrived. He wanted me to keep working hard for my grades and keep getting grades in the range of excellence.

My stand with teachers was not only due to academic excellence but also in the area of sports. I was a number one sprinter, relay finisher, sack racer, and a good rounders team player. I have fond memories of practicing for the sack race by running around the field beside my teacher, on whom I had a crush and felt good about the feedback he gave at the end of practice, "Good job, Florence!" Not even suspecting how I felt about him when I replied, "Thank you, Sir." In those days, I would just wear a cute smile and did not say much. I remember how proud the teachers were of me when I won my races and scored points for our *house*. Family members told me of the incident whereby one spectator in seeing me approach the starting line commented, "Where is that little fat girl going?" Before long, in seeing me ahead of the other athletes and hearing my relatives and friends rooting, "Go, Rita, go," they too joined in rooting me on. These memories make you cherish the teachers who prepared you for success back then and now.

Other ways in which I celebrated being the *teacher's pet* were in foreign language classes. I simply love languages. So back in high school, no sooner than we were taught vocabulary and grammar, I would write letters to the individual teachers in the language they taught. These were in French, Spanish, and Latin. I did not mind that the teacher would correct the letter and give it back to me. It was just one of my fun things to do while I learned. And today, I still love foreign languages and seek to learn different ones at every opportunity, although now I am my own teacher guided by the Mango Languages App. I totally enjoyed being the *teacher's pet* while that lasted!

Chapter 10

PREDICTIONS FOR WORK

In all my years of school, teachers gave me good reports. I basked in the *good name*. I thrived in the positivity of it all. Now I am in my last year of high school. All my teachers continue to write good reports and "a pleasure to teach," except the old English teacher who wrote, "She is too quiet in class. She will have problems in the working world." Although it was true of my quietness in class, I was very disappointed that he made that comment and, in my estimation, *spoiled* my good record!

I was now preoccupied with the thought. In my society, a quiet disposition was an honorable quality in a young lady. I interviewed and successfully held my first job as an interim teacher for one year, the proposed contract period. However, I did discover that my quietness worked both for and against me at different times. I found people were drawn to that quiet person in me because that gave them an opportunity to talk and express themselves freely while you listened most of the time. I decided people like to hear themselves talk, so I let them. On the other hand, I felt some amount of internal discomfort for not expressing myself more freely.

On to my second job as a records clerk in the public service, and I am still quiet by nature. Here at least two guys want to marry me. One is happy to make me know it's because I remind him of his "prim and proper Christian mother" and at least stop at my desk to make conversation. He knows because he is a divorcee, I am not interested. However, he is good at being friendly. The other guy is of Indian religion. I hardly talk with him when he approaches my desk, yet he asks the pandit on staff to talk with me on his behalf. This does not go well when the pandit relays to him my lack of interest, and he reveals how crestfallen he is by the defeated, depressed statement he makes to me.

I go on to other jobs later in my life and find a conglomeration of reactions toward me in the working world. In large part, people have shown me much appreciation and respect for my own demeanor and how I carry myself. But the few that have tried to scapegoat and demean have had a great negative impact on me while on the job. So, in a sense, my old English teacher had a point in saying I would have problems in the working world. He knew there were some mean people on the job out there. Although, I must say that in the midst of the challenges, I was able to find a way to overcome them, largely due to my Christian beliefs and training. That has contributed to great progress in my life. I did not have to be doomed for this prediction in my early life.

Chapter 11

MY LATE GREAT PARENTS

My parents were one in a million. They were a generation apart and were married for forty-seven years when my father died. They have both gone home to be with the Lord now, but they still and will always be with me in the Spirit. Dad was a very quiet gentleman, while Mom, although reserved, was somewhat more outgoing and extroverted. Although Dad was *a man of few words*, people often requested he be the master of ceremonies at their special functions such as weddings and twenty-first birthday celebrations. And he did an excellent job of keeping the program flowing nicely. In the face of differences, Dad would say, "I'm short, and my story is short." That was his way of refraining from getting into an argument. When Mom would pretend she was putting on boxing gloves and rolling up her sleeves, sparing in front of him, saying, "You have to beg me, 'Please, can we have a fight?'" Dad would smile, stop talking, and walk away. Mom was very humorous. That was her way of ending a possible dispute.

Both my parents were very ambitious individuals. They were ardent readers and read widely, including novels, books on religion, and medical books. They ensured we had copies of some of each in our home library, along with a collection of Webster's Encyclopedias and other reference journals. My parents did all they could to make necessary tools available to aid in our success in our own studies and also made themselves available to help and encourage us in our life's journey. When we stayed up studying and doing homework, Dad stayed up with us, providing moral support while he read a book, fed us *brain food* and a special cup of hot chocolate during our break time. Mom would listen to us read aloud while she worked on her sewing machine. She would ask us questions to check our comprehension and make comments to bring clarity. Amidst all this, both parents ensured they gave us positive feedback for a job well done!

My parents were very family-oriented and readily committed to family. In order to help his parents, as the eldest son, Dad left school at the age of fifteen and started a career in the postal service. He joined the public service as a mailman, received multiple promotions from senior postman to postmaster, and after forty-four consecutive years of service, he retired as Chief Postmaster of Guyana—a very prestigious position in our country. Meanwhile, Mom held her own in running her seamstress business from home. She was trained by the best from Paris and took pleasure in turning out both women's and men's clothing, including bridal gowns and outfits for the entire bridal party, and trained many young women in her trade. Mom was also honored to purchase an upright piano herself and put her children and grandchildren through music lessons. Despite her extremely busy schedule sewing for others, Mom made sure she sewed new clothing for her entire family every season. She also made crinoline hats and handbags for us girls and dashiki shirts for Dad and my brother. Further, she sewed a new outfit for herself for church every Sunday and refused to wear an outfit twice. She also outfitted the home with new curtains and chair covers that she sewed herself every quarter.

Despite their busy schedules, my parents made it possible to spend quality time with their children and grands. Dad knitted his own cast net and hammock. Then he took us fishing and crab catching. It was totally fascinating to watch Dad gather that cast net in one hand, lift it, bring it back, then cast it out, see it settle on the water in a circle, and disappear underwater, having been weighed down by the metal on the circumference of the net. As Dad drew the net in, we kids looked on in anticipation for the fruitful catch. Dad would educate us on the names of the fishes as he threw the little ones back so they could grow some more. On our return home, Dad cleaned, seasoned, and fried the fish himself. They were seasoned just right and tasted amazing, leaving a tantalizing aroma in the kitchen. Mom would complement Dad on his handy work while she made other dishes for the weekend meals. Very often, when Dad went fishing, he simultaneously set a trap for crabs. So, by the time we were ready to return home, Dad had quite a few crabs to go. We kids were instructed and made sure we stayed clear of their claws. But those too made a very tasty mouth-watering dish of curried crabs. Dad was an extraordinarily excellent cook, and many times he had friends over to share in his exceptional cuisine. Those were some super happy times!

Mom taught us every game she knew as a kid. It was so much fun playing ring games and hopscotch with Mom. Then later, Mom would be our best hands-on trainer for sports: track-and-field, hurdles, long jump, rounders, and cricket. Out of her wealth of wisdom, she would share all these tips to realize our success, and we did our best to comply. As expected, there were multiple cases of bruises and wounds to be dressed in the process, but we soon overcame those. Fun family times also took us to picnics in the park, where we would bring a huge pot of food and desserts to share, and we would play games and sports. Other remarkable fun times were when Dad took the family to cycle sports, and he would have to lift us young ones onto his shoulders to see above the crowd. Attendance at tea parties with Mom, participation in the plaiting of the maypole, and learning the common graces in sipping tea British-style.

Both my parents worked hard at passing the baton safely to us children. They worked well together to make it happen for us. Dad never forgot a birthday. He had every birthday written on the calendar each year, and with each new birth, he would add it to the calendar. He did the same with bills and so always paid bills on time. Notably, Dad bought everything in cash to avoid paying so much more in interest for the same item bought on terms. At the age of sixty-five, Dad bought his first car in cash, then learned to drive it so he could spare his family the angst of public transportation. After raising their own children, my parents helped to raise all their twenty-plus grandchildren.

Something I would always remember is how Dad made breakfast every Sunday morning when we were little. His omelet was thick and round like a large pizza, and it was a marvel to see it stay together and sliced so evenly. With every breakfast, Dad made eggnog from scratch. Along with this, we had Mom's pepper pot and homemade bread. She also was a remarkable cook, and we looked forward to Mom's splendid meals every day. Mom kept busy doing so much every day; she deserved the break on Sundays. We held Sabbath on Sundays, so after the family returned from the six o'clock Mass, we ate breakfast, and then the day was spent resting. No noisy playing on Sundays at our home. We did quiet things like reading a book. Then after dinner, before bedtime, the entire family did an evening devotional together. Each person read a portion of scripture consisting of Psalm 23 and Psalm 91, sang hymns, and prayed. Devotionals were coordinated by my parents and led by Dad. My parents truly did an excellent job of teaching us how to know, love, and serve God! For this, I shall be forever grateful.

Chapter 12

SIBLINGS

We siblings were six total and, to date, take great pleasure in befriending each other. Growing up, Mom encouraged us to play with each other in our own yard. She emphasized we were a large enough group to play various games among ourselves. From time to time, we would have friends over, but Mom always preferred we did the playing in our own domain. We kids did not mind this most of the time. Those who stepped out of bounds received just punishment, and the rest of us learned vicariously. As we grew, we learned it was not such a challenge getting parental permission to do things differently; you just had to ask and follow through on stipulated guidelines. We enjoyed doing things together as siblings and fell into three groups in the process: those who played hard, those who played safe, and those who dared to be different. My eldest baby sister and I were those who invariably played safe. We tried to do almost everything "by the book" as outlined by our parents, so it was not surprising we kept out of trouble with our parents, while other siblings had to be reined in every now and then.As children, we played well together and got along most of the time. Any differences were settled quickly and amicably. No one held grudges but stood up one for the other in times of challenge. When it came to family, our motto was "you touch one, you touch all!" And that alone warned other kids off from bothering us. Most everyone sought to be our friend. My brother and sister before me were the most popular, and if you saw me with a large number of children, it was their friends. Personally, I always had at least one friend, and when that person left, I had one new friend. My siblings were my friends, and they made good, faithful friends.

My eldest sister and I were almost always the ones with the most money because we saved some of every allowance our parents gave us and took every opportunity to save from gifts received from relatives and friends. We greatly enjoyed visits from those who dug deep in their pockets and came out with a fist full of money for us children to share. We also liked that they rotated who would be in charge of dividing and sharing the funds depending on their chronological age in the lineup of children. Each of us felt very important when it came to our turn. The best time was at Christmas when we would open our saving boxes to see how much we had saved over the year and what we could purchase with our money. One time, Merle and I pooled our resources to buy a baby stroller, while Patty and Pansy bought a bowlegged life-sized doll to put into the stroller. It was a very exciting time taking turns pushing the baby doll in the stroller!

My oldest sibling and only brother, Bert, was and still remains popular with the rest of us kids. He always looked out for us and stood up for our best interests. Even into my senior years, Bert has a special way of looking out for his baby sister by sharing encouraging forwards, clips and songs. "Uncle Bert," as we often refer to him out of respect, is very humorous and often has a funny story to share. Uncle Bert has a special love for horses and was mounted police for several years before coming to the United States. He is also a freelance painter who loves to gift his impromptu works of art, much to the joy of the receiver. Uncle Bert, like my parents, is very family-oriented and takes great pride in the accomplishments of his children and grands, who have made it to college, and has genuine positive feedback for those who work hard.

Merle, my eldest sister, is known best for her diligence in work. She has worked for over forty years as an educator, including serving as principal and training junior teachers for multiple years. She now works in the health field, providing quality care for seniors, and vows, "I'm retired but not tired." And the seniors appreciate her so much! Next in line is Sister Pat, who is known for *dotting her i's and crossing her t's*. She is also admired for her significant classy style of dressing. Sister Pat is your go-to person for editing your important document and/or paper. She has served as secretary of her church for over thirty years. Pansy is my popular sister who knows everyone and vice versa. She recently retired after working with CUNY Graduate Center for almost thirty years. Now she's vying for the Best Globetrotter Prize and doing well so far. Then there's my baby sister, Joy. I've deemed her my "best sibling prayer partner." Joy and I could pray about anything and everything! She also has worked with her company for over thirty years and is honored to be a go-getter and an ardent encourager.

My siblings and I have been proven to be the best friends one could ever have and want to have—another miracle!

Chapter 13

ALL MY CHILDREN

Motherhood is a wonderful experience. But when you get the privilege of parenting children without having to go through all the challenging process of bringing them into the world, you are blessed and *chosen*! I have never been married, never bore a child, yet I can say I have many children: some grown, others still growing and happy to call me "Mother," among other names like "Aunty" and fondly "AR." Where did all these children come from? My siblings, their children, and then some! That's right! I helped raise all my nieces and nephews and then some great-nieces and nephews. When kids saw us at school, they thought I was the children's grandmother and would call out to me as such. We did not stop to correct them—it did not matter!

The gathering of my children started when I was still in my mid-teens, and my siblings started their families. Because my siblings and their spouses both worked, it was difficult to find dependable childcare resources, so my parents offered to help with that role. Since I still lived at home, I became a natural part of the process and was happy to be my parents' right hand in helping to bring up the children. The Word says, "Train up a child in the way he should go, and when he is old, he will not depart from it" (Proverbs 22:6, NKJV), and so the children were off to a good start. From the cradle, I took them under my wing and taught them what I knew. From birth, the babies came to live with us. So I was able to do everything with and for them as any good parent would. This did not preclude their birth parents from playing their role. They had a very active part in the lives of their offspring. There were just more of us in the parenting role to help provide moral and communal support to the children and their parents. Those parents who could not come daily came weekly and were diligent in doing their part and bringing joy to the larger group. We had lots of fun doing things together. Interestingly, although the children were very dutiful to their biological parents, they were very committed to me. They were very respectful and, like I would say, acted as if they owned me. To date, most of them continue to act that way, showing love, regard, and due respect to their "aunty-mother." I myself use that term when reminding some I'm more than an aunt to them. However, it is a true blessing when a great-niece, Mickalla, could present you with a Mother's Day card that reads, "I'm honored to call you Mother!"

Every so often, some of the children and I would reminisce on activities we did together when they were young, and they would emphasize what they loved most. We truly enjoyed our time together: chore time and rewards, outings, and picnics in the park. Show of care and concern for me came in the face of a crisis. On one occasion, some of us were on a road trip and were involved in an auto accident. When the incident was reported back to the house, the children there were very concerned to know that their favorite aunty was alright. The parents also acknowledge the motherhood and qualities from my end and celebrate that. On one Mother's Day, one sister greeted me like this, "You are the Mother of all Mothers... M-u-d-d-e-r-s. You must be Abraham's sister... You have more children than everybody else... Happy Mother's Day!" Of course, this made for good humor, and we laughed heartily. But the more funny part is this: most of the children look like me as opposed to their birth parents.

Then there are others like my cousins and young friends who call me "Mom" out of fondness and respect. My children come in different ages, sizes, and shapes, but I am fond of them all. They often share about projects on which they are working and provide a running commentary on their progress and developments. I'm usually glad to participate in this way and happy that they see it fit to include me. On one occasion, my sister and I were talking with her son on the phone when he received a call on his other phone. We were both blessed to hear him tell the person, "I'm talking with my parents now. I'll call you back in a little while." It was significant that he said "parents." I do appreciate all my children and feel special when they seek me out to discuss important issues. God bless all my children!

On one occasion, my two young nieces and I were at a repast, having attended the funeral of a friend's husband. An older lady reached out to me across the table and offered, "Thanks for the good job you've done with the girls!" The conversation that ensued revealed she had been admiring the girls' good behavior and mannerisms from across the room and assumed I was their grandmother. On learning I was their great aunt, she was even more impressed and awe-struck. It is a true blessing to have been chosen to help raise all my children and to be a proven mother without birthing a child. God is good.

Awesome God we serve!

Chapter 14

How Would I Know?

Life can be tricky sometimes! How would I know you can enjoy your life without realizing all your dreams and goals as you know them?

At ages six and seven, my sister Pansy and I would take my mother's bridal fashion book and check off the bridal gowns we would like to wear for our wedding. Growing up, I thought that I would be married by age twenty-one. Twenty-one seemed a fascinating number since, at that time, it was the age of majority, the time when a young person received their own key to the parents' home. So for many reasons, it was a time to which you looked forward. But twenty-one came and went—no wedding— and so did multiple other ones. But how would I know I would still have a happy life? Just to take a stand, one day, I complained to a pastor friend, "What about me? Where is my husband? I've been a good girl... Where is my family?" Then I realized I have God, I have His son, Jesus, and I have the Holy Spirit all dwelling richly in me, and I have everything—my joy is full! My dreams and goals were based on societal ideals.

How would I know that working as a psychologist, psychotherapist, social worker, educator, and mentor can bring so much satisfaction? Although, a young client once said defensively to me, "You therapists are just nosey... You all just want to know people's business!" By the time I got to age sixty, I had held a "super bash" to mark that milestone, and as led by the Lord, I combined the celebration with an ordination service. This served for a very extraordinary celebration and better than the wedding to which I had looked forward. It was a very moving occasion when I committed to missionary service. God has made me happy in service in season and out of season, and I am pressing on. For me, every journey is a missionary journey. When I'm asked to do a message, I act as if it's my first and last opportunity with the intention that God gets all the glory. When people report being blessed by the Word, I know I did my part as I should.

And how would I know I would be in the Ministry, have so many friends, pray for so many people, and have so many people praying for me? How would I know I would have friendships that started in my earlier life last into my senior years and blossom into very pleasant, meaningful relationships whereby God is now using me to be an encouragement to those who encouraged me? In youth, our youth leaders at church were very precious to us. We looked up to them and sought counsel from them in times of distress. When I was young, my own youth leaders took me to our beautiful botanical gardens, where they patiently listened to my woes and prayed with me. Little did we know that after so many years, she and I would be talking woman to woman and praying about routine life issues now that her partner has gone to be with the Lord. She doesn't even remember half the things they did for me in my youth... How would I know it could be like this?

The Mid-Times

Chapter 15

COMING TO CHRIST

I believe I came to know Christ as my Savior at an early age—around ages three to ten. My mom recounted stories of my returning home from Sunday school and inviting her to pray. I would encourage her to repeat The Lord's Prayer after me. I was not satisfied with the mundane way she would say the prayer and would ask her to repeat it in the same animated way in which I said it. Mom said it made her laugh, but she noted I reminded her of her own grandmother, who was a faith healer on whom many called in times of sickness and challenges. So she observed me following that trend as I grew up.

At that period of my life, I do recall paying strict attention in Sunday school, at family devotions, and as my parents trained us. I internalized almost everything well and strove to do everything to the best of my ability to follow guidelines. That was to please and make God happy. I wanted to be just like His Son, Jesus, after accepting Him into my little heart. When I was afraid, I would repeat the twenty-third Psalm quietly to myself, and that would help me get through the challenge. I read my little Gideon Testament regularly outside of family devotions without being prompted by my parents or anyone else. I was a little believer living for the Lord and wanted my life to tell. So, I was not just a well-behaved child; I was a Christian walking the walk, although I did not do much of the talk.

My parents' consistent positive feedback on my good behavior helped me to aspire even more to maintain that status quo and all contributed to my excelling both behaviorally and academically. As my mom put it, "You do so well at everything you put your hand to do." Later on, I discovered that line in the Bible as a description of those who live close to the Lord (Deuteronomy 15:10). The Lord had established His hold on my life, and I had claimed the victory in Him from that early age!

Chapter 16

RENEWAL OF VOWS

At age sixteen, I rededicated my life to Christ. I had followed in a close step while walking with the Lord. I read my Bible every day on awakening and before going to bed. My routine was to complete all my homework, study all my subjects, then read from the New Testament in addition to Psalms and Proverbs. Further, I sought every opportunity to apply the Word to my life. I had learned this little verse which I put into action:

HOW TO READ THE BIBLE

Read it through

Dig it up

Pray it in

And live it out

As I went along, I thought I was doing quite well. I was now the secretary and librarian of our Bible club at high school. Bible Club met on Tuesdays after school. On this beautiful Tuesday afternoon, on or around June 6, 1966, we had a guest speaker. His name was Tom Skinner. He was an evangelist from the United States of America. It was a very exciting time for us at the Bible Club! Quite a good number of us were in attendance in the auditorium. Mr. Skinner preached a very stirring message, and in closing, he extended an invitation for people to stand if they wanted to accept Christ as their Savior. I remained seated because I knew I had already done so. Several students had stood up, but I stayed seated. By this time, Mr. Skinner had thrown out the invitation a second time. I still sat because I had already accepted Christ as Savior and was living earnestly for Him. At this time, Mr. Skinner gave the invitation again, adding, "If you want to be sure to be saved..." I continued to sit, but before realizing it, I was on my feet.

It was in later years that I realized that the Holy Spirit had put me on my feet like He did the prophet in Ezekiel 2:2 (also Ezekiel 3:24), and it was to bring me along my spiritual journey. Dr. Janice Thom-Collins, who was our Bible Club sponsor, counseled me using *The Romans Road to Salvation*:

"For all have sinned, and come short of the glory of God"
(Romans 3:23, KJV)

"For the wages of sin is death..."
(Romans 6:23, KJV)

"But God demonstrates His love for us in this: While we were still sinners, Christ died for us"
(Romans 5:8, NIV)

"For God so loved the world that he gave his only-begotten Son, that whoever believes in him shall not perish, but have eternal life"
(John 3:16, EHV)

"But as many as received him, to them gave he power to become the sons of God, even to them that believe on his name" (John 1:12, KJV). "That if thou shalt confess with thy mouth the Lord Jesus, and shalt believe in thine heart that God hath raised him from the dead thou shalt be saved. For with the heart man believeth unto righteousness; and with the mouth confession is made unto salvation"
(Romans 10:9–10, KJV)

The punchline here for me was Romans 10:9–10. I needed to tell others of my salvation, and although I was a quiet, reserved person, I should not keep it to myself. True, my behavior was reflective of who I was, but I also needed to speak of it and witness for Christ so others could get an opportunity to know Him too. As soon as I arrived home that day, I told my family of my unique experience at Bible Club, and since then, I have sought to maximize my opportunities to tell of God and salvation through Jesus the Christ. Thus, through the years, God has brought me progressively along as He has helped me to be more and more expressive in telling of Him and His word, including presentation of messages to large groups,

The Holy Spirit had put me on my feet all those years ago to realize all that God is doing in and through me in the ministry today!

Chapter 17

WATER BAPTISM

At about age seventeen, I signed up with the Brethren Church at Camp Street to attend classes in preparation for baptism by immersion. This is where we participated in Youth Fellowship and where my counselor had her church membership. So I was encouraged it would be a safe place to learn and grow further in things of a spiritual nature. Here at Bethel Gospel Hall, I was assigned into the capable hands of an older female counselor by the name of Mrs. Ruby Clarke. Now, Sister Clarke was also a mother-in-law to my sister Pat so this proposed to be a very trustworthy relationship.

"Mother Clarke," as we called her, was very patient in imparting knowledge and wisdom to me. She showed me from scripture verses the reasons for being baptized as in Romans 6:3–4, which stipulates as we go down into the waters of baptism, we demonstrate that we are buried with Christ, and as we arise out of these waters, we testify that we are raised up to live a new life in Christ, to walk as a child of light doing what glorifies God in all areas of our lives. She further showed that it was significant to have a large amount of water in order to be able to go down into it and be covered (John 3:23). Moreover, she made reference to scripture that verified that John was baptized where there was much water and that Jesus, our Savior Himself, submitted to this form of baptism (Matthew 3:13–17). Mother Clarke also taught me the graces of Christian living and how to conduct oneself in the church services, taking a humble seat until called up higher. I truly thank God for the memory of Mother Clarke and all she did to prepare me for water baptism and life in Christ!

But now, there was a hitch. My dear father, who was raised and raised us children in the Anglican Church, seemed to feel slighted that I was choosing to get baptized in another church which appeared he did not give me a "good enough" spiritual path. Well, in fact, Dad and Mom did a great job raising us spiritually. This I tried to relay to him. I was seeking to be obedient in stepping into the waters of baptism as a good witness. But Dad remained quiet as per his nature, and I felt hurt because I had hurt my father's feelings. I felt a need for Dad's blessing to pursue my goal. So I asked Mother Clarke to talk with Dad. She and her husband visited our home and talked with Dad, but he remained quiet. He did not voice one way or another whether I should go ahead with my plans. So here I was in limbo and feeling sadly ambivalent.

The day for scheduled baptisms arrived. I put on my white dress but arrived at church without a change of clothes, towel, and other preparations. When I talked with Mother Clarke, she was very disappointed when she learned that after months of taking classes in preparation for this special day, I was not going forward in taking this very meaningful step. She said, "Florence, are you going to sit by and watch the other candidates go down and not do it? It's as easy as kissing hands!"

It's like Mother Clarke said some magic word. My spirit was lifted, and my mind made up. The moment I shared with my sister Merle that I was going to be baptized, she quickly ran home and returned with the necessary change of clothing and other paraphernalia and seemed so happy for me—bless her heart! I stepped down into the waters of baptism, and it was remarkable. When Brother Ramsey lowered me into the water and brought me back up, a steady peace washed over me and remained with me for a very long time...I had taken a very significant step in my spiritual walk, and all was well. The scripture I was given on the occasion of my baptism was John 15:16, read by Bro. James: "Ye have not chosen me, but I have chosen you, and ordained you, that ye should go and bring forth fruit, and that your fruit should remain: that whatsoever ye shall ask of the Father in my name, he may give it you" (John 15:16, KJV).

I have hidden that scripture in my heart and cherish it for life and am reminded multiple times in testing situations that God Himself chose and ordained me. What a miracle!

Chapter 18

CALL TO SERVICE: DREAMWORK

I love the Lord dearly and have lived for Him and walked with Him from childhood. I have participated in spiritual activities at church, at school, at home, and in the community. There was no doubt in my mind that I was serving God in all these ways. However, one night, I had an experience that would, thereafter, clinch it for all time as I was directly called to service. It was a dream!

I found myself in the midst of a very large number of people in an area which could have been our National Park in Georgetown. Everyone seemed busy going to-and-fro. The large majority of people wore civilian clothing, but a smaller number were dressed in white shirts and black pants or skirts. These persons appeared to be the officials at this humongous event. At first, everything seemed splashed before me like a huge display, and a particular street sign caught my attention. It read, "*Sic ut tu servus est.*" Even in the dream, I was taken by that message and the busyness of the entire scenery. Later, I was walking in a mobile building unit when I walked close to one of the male officials who was going in the opposite direction.

On or around eight o'clock the next morning, I was doing my devotions and reading my bible when I heard a knock at our front door. I went to the door to find a stranger, but he was the official from my dream. Also, he was dressed as in the dream. He introduced himself as Pastor Tony Fontanelle and stated that my sister Patty had asked him to deliver an envelope from New York. I invited him in, and we talked briefly. Then I disclosed that he had been in my dream the night before. Since we had never met before, we both found this quite interesting, and he wanted to hear details of the dream. On hearing more of the dream, Pastor Tony drawled, "Well... glory to God," then shared that the dream was *confirmation* of the reason he had come to Guyana. He further explained that God had asked him to gather the leaders of the churches in Guyana for a Body of Christ conference and for them to, corporately, pray for the country.

Now I was grappling with my message from the dream. *Sic ut tu servus est.* Very readily, based on my little foreign language skills, I could tell it was telling me to serve; but the word "*sic*" was very unfamiliar to me, so I looked it up in the Webster dictionary. There I was enlightened that it was a Latin word that, when used at the beginning of a statement, makes it a command. So, no ands, ifs, or buts, that statement was saying, "You serve." Therefore, I was commissioned in the dream to serve. Consequently, when asked by Pastor Tony to help coordinate the first Crusade, I served willingly, cheerfully, and with a knowledge that I had been divinely commissioned!

As providence would have it, I continue to serve in the same spirit but with more knowledge that God works in a mysterious way his wonders to perform, and I can discern his leading and prompting to service in whatever mode it comes—dream or no dream—I've been called and commissioned to service once and for all time!

Chapter 19

HOLY SPIRIT BAPTISM

It happened with a burst of light and the words, *"Eli...Eli...Lama Sabachthani ta!"* Thus, I had experienced the baptism of the Holy Spirit with the evidence of *speaking in tongues.* These words came from me audibly without any effort on my part. I had been kneeling beside my bed in the hotel room where I was attending a Believers' Conference. Alone in my room, I felt led to spend some time looking to the Lord. Just minutes before, I heard someone enter the room, and I, naturally, looked up, but no one was there. So I resumed my prayer posture and continued praying. Now, I was consumed with awe and wonderment. I never thought this was how it would happen for me... by myself in a strange land in a hotel room! I was overjoyed and kept praising and thanking God for blessing me with this experience.

My very first exposure to people in church speaking in tongues was at the Assemblies of God Church I visited at about age thirteen. I had been a rapt worshipful participant and enjoyed the service until several in the congregation began speaking in tongues. Almost immediately, I became a spectator. This was all new for me, and I was sure they had learned and spouted whatever they were saying that I did not understand. Then I read about it in the Bible myself. Mark 16:17 (NIV) says, "And these signs will accompany those who believe: In my name, they will drive out demons; they will speak in new tongues..."

Acts 2:4 (NIV) quotes, "All of them were filled with the Holy Spirit and began to speak with other tongues as the Spirit enabled them."

Acts 19:6 reports (NIV), "When Paul placed his hand on them, the Holy Spirit came on them, and they spoke in tongues and prophesied."

I started to get an understanding that the phenomenon of speaking in tongues is a spiritual experience to be had and one not to be taken lightly.

I had yet to experience this act, so when earlier in the session, the preacher gave an invitation for people who wanted to have this experience to stand for prayer, I readily complied. The session had been over for a couple of hours now, but God answered prayers, and in His time, He granted my request. Now I was both water-baptized and Holy Spirit-filled with the evidence of speaking in tongues, and it all happened in my own privacy—true to form of how I preferred things to be done at that time. Surely, God is a good God, and He does not seek to embarrass us.

Ever since that faith-stirring day, I have sought to learn more of the working of the Holy Spirit and also taught about it. I have prayed openly in tongues as led by the Spirit and based on the guidelines of the word. Now I feel I have *seen it all*, Spirit-wise, and I just have to flow in the Spirit! Like the Negro Spiritual says, "When the Spirit says dance, I will dance... When the Spirit says sing, I will sing..." The scripture says it is better to obey God rather than man (Acts 5:29).

Chapter 20

SPECIAL DIRECT ASSIGNMENT

I had just attended a week-long believer's conference. I had seen visions, dreamed dreams, and experienced the baptism of the Holy Spirit with the evidence of speaking in tongues. Now I was sitting on a jet plane flying from Nassau, Bahamas, to New York City. Led by the Lord, I had done a devotional reading of Ezekiel 2–3 and was quietly praying and meditating on the scriptures when the Lord spoke to me. He said very distinctly and calmly, "I have a work for you to do in New York." Immediately, I recognized this was God. I knew I was not talking to myself, and I was not hearing voices... It was an awesome experience!

First of all, I realized we do not speak like that. "I have a work for you to do..." This caught my attention and soon became a conversation that included topics like make-up and portion control. The gist of this dialogue bordered on moderation in doing things, and several years later, as I saw these become headlines in the media and community, I reflected on my earlier communication with God and noted that it was a part of him preparing me for *the work*. But let me say that the make-up issue was revealed almost immediately because as soon as I landed in New York and greeted my then fifteen-year-old niece, Sharon, her response was a complaining, "Aunty... you have on too much make-up!" Right away, I remembered my conversation with the Lord. Things were falling into place very quickly.

However, for three days, I pondered and prayed about the experience of God talking to me. It was my first experience of this kind. I had not told anyone about it either, not even Brother Matthew

Allen, who sat next to me, making light conversation later. I had not mentioned it to any of my family members either, although my mother and sister, Pat, were readily accessible. On this third evening, as I spoke with the Lord in prayer before retiring to bed, I asked Him to confirm what He told me on the plane through Pastor Bertril Baird. Now Pastor Baird was one of the Keynote presenters at the Bahamas Conference and had adopted me as his spiritual daughter during that week. At this time, he was also one of two main speakers for a week-long Crusade being held at the church my sister attended. So far, I had not told Pastor Baird about that unique experience on the plane. I was just grappling with it before God.

The following evening after the service, I stood visiting with my mother, sister, and some pastors as we waited to return home. Pastor Baird had been the preacher this evening and now joined us where we stood fellowshipping. He greeted the others in a normal manner, but when he spoke with me, he said, "Sister Flo, the Lord has called you to be a missionary in New York." Head bent on one side, in my quiet way, I replied, "Thank you, Pastor Baird." And he continued, "So radiate... A lot of people out there need you!" With that, I smiled. God had confirmed what He told me on the plane through my adopted spiritual dad, Pastor Baird, just like I had asked Him to do!

It was only days later, at the end of the Crusade, that I sought out Pastor Baird and shared with him my unique experience on the plane and the special, direct assignment from my Father God. Pastor Baird then was able to provide brief counsel, encouraging me on how to proceed. Basically, he said, "Don't be timid... Continue to trust and follow God in all He tells you to do. Join a local church and work out of there." To date, although my adopted dad has gone to be with the

Lord, I, prayerfully, continue to follow that guideline, and much of my missionary work is centered in New York and its environs!

Chapter 21

TO THE UTTERMOST PARTS

My very first missionary project was located at my sister's home church. They were preparing to implement an elementary school program. The Monday following the end of the Crusade, the pastor's wife made telephone contact and requested that I assist them with this project. I helped them write up the curriculum and assisted with grade four for approximately one month until their assigned teacher could arrive from another state. Then, for another month, I assisted with pre-K and kindergarten. I was happy to be of service wherever there was a need and felt quite fulfilled knowing that I was walking as supernaturally guided in divine instruction. Once everything was established and the school was off to a good start, I moved over to a neighboring church school, where I assisted in organizing the books in their library and with clerical duties in their office.

All the while, I kept before God concerning the work to which He had assigned me in New York. I had multiple questions, such as am I to stay in New York for the rest of my life? If not, how do I know when it is appropriate to move on? That is when God reminded me of Jesus' instructions to the disciples in Acts 1:8 (KJV), "But ye shall receive power, after the Holy Ghost has come upon you: and ye shall be witnesses unto me both in Jerusalem, and in all Judea, and in Samaria, and unto the uttermost part of the earth."

Now the picture was becoming clearer. As led by the Holy Spirit, I understood that just as the disciples were to witness to their local communities and other extended populations and places, so too were I to attend to God's work in many places as He led me. This included far and near places and whatever the needs were to be addressed as led by God. It was a new teaching/learning experience for me, but I was willing to go the course and distance with God's help and guidance. God was faithful. He led me every step of the way.

Upon completion of a master's degree in Psychology at Hunter College in New York, the Lord led me back to Virginia, where I had completed a bachelor's degree many years before. I lived in the same little college town where I had attended school and taught at a nearby Community College. Simultaneously, I attended the same church and sang in the same choir. But this time around, I was also serving as film representative for a Christian organization called "Underground Evangelism." My task here was to present a film describing the needs and work surrounding people in the Communist Bloc countries and pick up a free-will offering to be used for printing and distributing Bibles, other Christian literature, food, and medical supplies to the people there.

When I went on my first assignment with Underground Evangelism, I was quietly elated when the host at the little country church greeted me with a smile.

"Are you the missionary?"

It was the first time since my supernatural assignment that anyone had addressed me using that title... I felt like a connection was made within me, and the plot was thickening. I looked forward to going to the uttermost parts of the earth with God's work!

Camps and Shenanigans

Chapter 22

MAKING OF A MISSIONARY

From an early age, one could tell I was destined to be a servant of God—a missionary. I was very pious and obedient. Others might not have realized it, but I was living out my salvation as I saw, felt, and understood it. I sought to please God in all I did. Whether I was successful or not remains to be answered, but I understood that the blood of Jesus prevails in the midst of my challenges and is sufficient to pay the price for my forgiveness where I fall short. I did not always match this concept with my performance as I was very perfectionistic and felt I had to do and have everything correct, but with time, prayers, spiritual education, awareness, and development, I got it. It was not so much about me but what Jesus Christ had done for me by dying in my place on the cross...it was not about my good works (Ephesians 2:8–10).

At every stage of my life, you could trace the development of missionary service. In the Bible Club at high school, I served as secretary and librarian. I wrote letters to request and arrange for weekly speakers and provided timely feedback to our sponsor and oversight committee. As the librarian, I kept a close monitor over our mobile book unit to ensure the whereabouts of each book in our small collection. This type of activity kept me focused and encouraged as I served in these meaningful ways and experienced the appreciation of our unified community.

With the developments surrounding my water and Holy Spirit baptisms, it is clear that a higher power was operating in the midst. The diligence of my counselor in preparing me for water baptism and ensuring that I followed through was remarkable, and the spontaneous willingness of my sister to hurry home to get the change of clothing and other items I needed was something of a miracle waiting to happen. Everything simply came together like a puzzle! And my dad was alright... my getting baptized in another church denomination did not have any ulterior effects on him. I was definitely relieved. The major issue is that I did not want to offend my dad, but that was soon behind us, and we proceeded with the same harmonious spirit as we did before, which made all the difference to me. Further, the dramatic experience of Holy Spirit baptism was not expected but welcomed. With this development came a sure boldness that I lacked before as I shared the Gospel.

Every step of the way, I see that God was preparing me for the journey and, simultaneously, using me in His work. Added to this was the spiritual grooming at Youth Fellowship on Fridays. I particularly enjoyed the evangelistic movies describing missionary doctors traveling to remote places to bring the Gospel. It was at those times I knew I wanted to be a missionary doctor too. Also, a great influence was the committed, faithful, Christian spirit of the members of my church home. Certainly not to forget the early grooming by Dad and Mom when they awakened all their children at four in the morning to prepare for six o'clock Mass at our little Anglican Church about two miles away, and the family devotion time, when we would sing hymns, and each family member would read a portion of scripture from the Bible. This practice included the youngest to the oldest family member. It was a blessed time on which I reflect with much appreciation.

Added to all this was the ability to see my parents—imperfect as they were—live an exemplary, balanced Christian life before us. Our entire family attended church together each week. We all participated in church concerts, tea parties, bring-and-buy sales, and other family activities.

When doing household chores, it was fantastic to see Mom wash and Dad dry dishes before putting them away. In addition, it was very rewarding to watch Dad bring Mom a glass of water without being asked because he knew she kept so busy and would overlook her water intake. Furthermore, it was a delight to watch Mom's appreciative facial expression when Dad would supply a much-needed sewing needle when she could not find one. He would have found and kept a needle safe, knowing this time would come!

It was also good to see our parents have fun with close friends and other family members. Cycle sports, plays at the local community center, and plaiting of the maypole are some other fun activities our family enjoyed together. It was a very timely learning experience to see our parents get along with others, as well as to see them do good for others. Mom was often sewing clothing for people without payment, and one of Dad's young workers vowed he would always remember Dad's kindness in allowing him time off for studies when he needed to prepare for examinations.

All these influences went into preparing and making me the missionary I am today, praise God!

Chapter 23

QUIET TIME

Camp taught us many meaningful Christian values. A very critical one was the habit of spending quality time with God on awakening every day, preferably before getting into other activities. At camp, this was referred to as "quiet time." Each morning, campers were encouraged to spend time individually and in small groups reading a portion of scripture, discussing and praying about it, then putting it into practice in their lives. Small groups consisted of six to eight participants who shared a cabin which was supervised by a camp counselor. Males and females used separate cabins.

Scriptures and topics for quiet time were based on the theme for camp on a particular occasion. Each small group would do quiet time in their individual cabin, and on meeting in the larger group, an agreed-on volunteer would present brief feedback on what transpired during quiet time that day. This approach contributed to creating interesting dialogue in exploring God's Word, as well as keeping us, youngsters, alert and focused on the spiritual aspects of our lives. Everyone was given an opportunity to participate in either reading the scriptures and/or sharing their thoughts and understanding on the subject. Consequently, it was easy to think, ponder and pray, as well as practice biblical concepts learned throughout the day. One catchy slogan of quiet time was, "Seek God in the morning, and you'll have Him through the day!"

As we internalized the wise counsel in the concept of quiet time, many of us continued this healthy, spiritual practice on return to our homes. Personally, I did quiet time both on awakening in the morning and last thing before going to bed at night. I found this time with God and in His presence very fascinating and combined it with my little ditty on how to read the Bible:

Read it through

Dig it up

Pray it in

And live it out!

To date, I continue to find spending a quiet time with our Heavenly Father both in the morning and at night to be a very rewarding spiritual practice. It provides you a sense of belonging as you get direction from above. You tend to hear God better and more readily in your quiet time with Him. You find that certain closeness, joy, and peace with *Our Father who art in heaven*, and you *hallow His name*. Some encourage—and I highly recommend—that you also select a special quiet place for these prized moments and sessions with Papa.

Chapter 24

BIRTHDAYS

Birthdays are very special occasions in our family. My dad took the time to remember the birthday of each family member, including the grandchildren. He purchased each card himself and would be sure to put some money inside. This made for some extremely excited, happy recipients and a fun time for everyone present. A special practice was where Dad would be fattening a live chicken, duck, or turkey weeks and/or months ahead of the occasion to have it ready to be cooked and eaten on the special day. Typical special birthday dishes included curry and roti, macaroni and cheese, chow mein, patties, cheese straw, birthday cake, and homemade ice cream, which almost everyone was happy to take a turn churning. Our parents, certainly, went to all lengths to make birthdays memorable for us. Yet, I looked forward to spending birthdays at camp!

My birthday came around Easter on many occasions, and along with my sister, Pansy, I would be at Easter Camp. Those were some of the most enjoyable times in my life. Since camps were held during the school vacation, we were given the opportunity to attend camp during the Easter and summer vacations, and as we grew into adulthood, there was an opportunity to attend a weekend camp at other times during the year. Most times, this would be held during a holiday weekend. But Easter Camp was almost always the best. Perhaps it was because it was my birthday and I would become sentimental. Perhaps I was associating the Easter sunrise service with new beginnings where I, too, was experiencing new beginnings as I entered a new year in my life. It was a joyful yet sobering time. We would celebrate how Christ rose from the grave, and we, too, will rise on our resurrection morning. It gave us hope and a future. It was refreshing to be born around such a critical time of importance to us, Christians, and the church. Again, this was an experience that made you feel a closeness to God the Father, Son, and Holy Spirit!

Of course, another high point of being at camp on your birthday was when so many people would dote on you—take the time to greet you once word got out that you had a birthday—and the large group would sing the good old Happy Birthday song while you blushed. You might even get an impromptu birthday cake! The sessions at camp took on a different meaning for you. Everything became more important, and you remembered them more readily and for a longer time. You would miss your family, but it was okay. You had *family* here, and it was a different, broadening of your horizons kind of experience. You made special connections with others who shared your birth date and/or month, and you looked forward to celebrating with them the following year. You made lasting friends of these individuals and remembered them for years to come when your birthdays rolled around. In addition, you got many people praying over you, and you just felt your blessings flow. Those were *the good old days* of birthdays at camp!

Chapter 25

THE VISION

This turned out to be an eventful day at camp. The preacher was sharing from John 15 about Jesus Christ being the vine and His followers being the branches. I sat there paying rapt attention, prayerfully, listening when I got a vision. It was a picture of a branch with the seemingly most perfect green leaves. Those leaves were so alive and healthy; they looked very inviting! I marveled at receiving this vision as it was in public, and it came in the midst of a camp session of the larger group, and everyone was in the Main Hall at this time.

Very readily, I could identify with the message. In keeping with the text, I could tell that without Christ, we are nothing and could do nothing. In addition, in Christ and as followers of Christ, God wants us to be healthy branches and bear good fruit. Based on the vision, it seems like we were getting there and needed to keep working towards that goal. I continued to listen as I prayed and pondered about the vision, not knowing it was something I would be required to share with this large group.

Before the session ended, as the preacher wrapped up his message, he announced that someone got a vision for the group. Being new to all these developments, I waited to see if anyone else would share. As no one else did, I stood up and revealed what I had seen in the vision.

Immediately, you could detect surprise in members of the group. The preacher discussed the significance of the vision and encouraged the group to seek and stay close to God to realize His purposes in being healthy branches that bear fruit.

This message was well received by the campers, and an immediate surge of enthusiasm was detected as the session ended. It was evident that people had questions about whom God chose to give the vision. Every little group you walked past was discussing the vision.

Personally, I could understand their questioning as far as whom God chooses to give the vision since, under normal circumstances, I never had much to say. My personality was that of a more reserved, reticent nature. So, it was obvious that God uses whom and what He wishes for His own purposes to be realized, and He does so whenever He wishes. My own observation also would be that God would seek to use someone who was earnestly seeking Him as I was doing throughout the session.

One thing that stood out concerning the giving of the vision and the multiple questions was that other people don't have to know you, and you don't have to be loud and outspoken for God to use you. He can use even an otherwise quiet, shy person when He wants to get His work done!

Chapter 26

INSEPARABLE SIBLINGS

Another issue of some interest to campers was that my sister and I were always together. Many, including leadership members, asked if we were twins and were surprised to learn that we were not. We even dressed alike. Our parents had raised us to have a close relationship and to look out for each other. So being at camp was no different. We stayed together and lent support to one another. If anything, we were a good example of faithfulness and commitment. Nevertheless, Pastor Paul thought they would have to find a way of separating us so we could mingle and interact more with the rest of the group. We had no problem with that, but at every opportunity, we came back together—inseparable siblings. In time, the larger population seemed to accept that they had to receive us the way that we were.

In time, others seemed to realize that the saying of two heads being better than one did not only apply to married couples and marveled that as siblings, we got along so well. I think our behavior and relationship caused other siblings there to examine their own relationship and to seek to do better with one another. We were a team within a team, and that was good for us. We wanted to be a good example to others, and so we rallied on.

Of course, we also wanted to view things from the perspective of others and did our best to mingle and mix. Although I did not have much to say, I provided a good listening ear for those who did and ensured they knew I was listening and interested in what they had to say. On the other hand, my sister was very friendly and outgoing, so she never had problems making new friends who also became my friends. So, in a sense, we had our own scheme of socializing and making others feel appreciated and friend-worthy. In some ways, I think camp leaders realized this fact which made them feel more at ease. Going forward, they no longer had to worry about us—the inseparable Fraser siblings!

Chapter 27

RESPECT

I have great respect for those who seek to know, love, and serve God. I thank God for my parents, who were the first individuals to teach us, their children, to do just that. Many people still need to know there is a vast difference between knowing about God and actually knowing God. We can know God as a person with whom we have a personal relationship. When God created man in His own image and breathed His own breath into him, they had a close relationship until man disobeyed God, and this sin caused a great division separating God and man (Genesis 3:7–10; 22–24). Thereafter, every person born has been labeled a "sinner" and considered separated from God (Romans 3:23) until they take specific steps to bridge the gap back to God.

Adam and Eve showed disrespect when they disobeyed God and ate from the tree of knowledge of good and evil, so God banished them from the Garden of Eden. But God also created a master plan for how men, women, and children can be brought back to the right relationship with God. He set things up so that His Son Jesus, the Christ, would die in our place since "the wages of sin is death; but the gift of God is eternal life in Jesus Christ our Lord" (Romans 6:23). When we accept God's plan and take Jesus Christ as our Savior, we're able to get back into a good relationship with God. He becomes Our Father, and we become His children (John 1:12).

When we have and show respect for God, we tend to have and show more respect one to the other. Love for God influences a love for each other that blooms and bears natural respect. First John 3:18

(NLT) encourages, "Dear children, let's not merely say that we love each other; let us show the truth by our actions."

Being respectful becomes a part of our character as we practice reflecting on God and Christ. This good characteristic can also keep us in good standing with those in authority and as we communicate with others. Everyone likes to be respected, even if they fall short at times. So, despite the lack of perfection on our part, we should strive to show respect and, in turn, get respect from others.

When we know, love, and serve God, we develop special respect for God that more readily spreads to others as we seek to please God in our daily lives and activities. *Respect* is a very critical part of our Christian profile!

Chapter 28

ALL FOR JESUS

Throughout my life, I have been committed to living for Christ. I have thought long and hard before speaking lest I sin with my words and bring pain to someone and, by so doing, dishonor God (Psalm 39). I have done my best to live peacefully with all men. In everything, I have sought to bring glory to the God I serve. I want my life to tell for Jesus, still. I want my life to shine like a bright light in the darkness of this world. Matthew 5:13–20 encourages us to be the salt of the earth, whereby if we lose our edge, there will be no saltiness, and to be the light of the world which, if hidden, there will only be darkness. Hence, we want to be a good, positive influence on our community and the world around us.

When people witness our good works, they must glorify the God we serve and desire to serve Him too (Matthew 5:15–16). My own desire is to be obedient to the great commission in Matthew 28:18–20, going into all the world and making disciples of all men, ensuring that people know the one and true living God who wants to save them and who has made every provision for them to be saved from the consequences of their own sins and hence gain heaven instead of hell. We want to do everything as unto the Lord with all cheerfulness and in good spirit (Colossians 3:23–25).

I want every area of my life to reflect Christ and that my life is hidden with Christ in God (Colossians 3:3). That would be a great testimony if only I were perfect, but my perfection is in Christ. As Philippians 3:12 (NASB1995) says, "Not that I have already obtained it or have already become perfect, but I press on so that I may lay hold of that for which also I was laid hold of by Christ Jesus."

As I seek to give all for Jesus, these desires might not be easy to live out, but when we put our faith and trust in God and seek to do all things in His strength, these things can become a reality. Philippians 4:13 (NKJV) predicts, "I can do all things through Christ who strengthens me."

So, as for me, I'm pressing on in Jesus. As I close these chapters, I recommit my life to Him and invite you to do the same. Or, if you have not accepted Jesus Christ as Savior, do so now and experience that wonderful new life in Christ, whereby you too can experience multiple miracles from heaven!

ABOUT THE AUTHOR

Rev. Dr. Florence Fraser has been in the Ministry for most of her life. She accepted Christ as Savior at an early age and renewed that decision in her teens. She is a water-baptized, Holy Spirit-filled intercessor and professionally ordained minister described by some as having "a quiet dynamism" in promoting God's kingdom through prayer and godly counsel. Her objective is to use God's Word, the Bible, to successfully pass the baton to the next generation.

Ms. Fraser's strong spiritual stand can be credited to her consistent godly upbringing by committed parents, regular participation in her local church, and active memberships in God-centered groups at high school and college. These include the Inter-school/Inter-Varsity Christian Fellowship (IS/IVCF), where she served as a camper, secretary, librarian, and sponsor, and the Student Committee on Religious Activities (SCRA), where she served as Chair of the Crisis Committee.

With a bachelor's degree in Psychology, a master's degree with concentration in Clinical Psychology, and a doctoral degree in Theocentric Psychology, Rev. Flo has positively impacted multiple lives, including the developmentally disabled, while working as a psychologist, social worker, psychotherapist in private practice in New York City and Georgia. As a trained mediator, she has traveled and trained in Mediation and Conflict Resolution in Virginia and neighboring states. In addition, she has presented at Women's Ministry Conferences and continues to provide godly counsel and mentoring through Fraser Family-Ministries International.

Further, Ms. Fraser has taught Nursery through University both in Guyana and the USA and counts it an honor to have taught college-level Psychology to the granddaughter of the late renowned radio and TV evangelist, Rev. Dr. Billy Graham. Despite traveling widely in Guyana, Suriname, the Caribbean, and North America, Dr. Fraser's most awesome reflection is that when her mother heard she had the opportunity to shake hands with Rev. Dr. Billy Graham, she quipped, "Now you know you don't wash that hand!"

Lightning Source UK Ltd.
Milton Keynes UK
UKHW051959100223
416857UK00019B/214